The River Will Save Us

Also by Linda Simone
Archeology
Cow Tippers
Moon: A Poem

The River Will Save Us

poems by

Linda Simone

Kelsay Books

© 2018 by Linda Simone. All rights reserved. This material may not be reproduced in any form, published, reprinted, recorded, performed, broadcast, without the express written consent of Linda Simone. All such actions are strictly prohibited by law.

Kelsay Books
Aldrich Press

502 S 1040E
A119
American Fork, Utah
84003

www.kelsaybooks.com

ISBN: 978-1-949229-07-3

First Edition
Printed in the United States of America

Cover design: Shay Culligan
Cover art: "River of Dreams," watercolor by Linda Simone

*For San Antonio,
the Jingu family,
Joe, Justin, and Nicole, my family,
and for Dreamers everywhere*

Contents

Poet Is a River (excerpt)

Postcard from a Past Life

The River Sings	17
Migration	19
Crossing 43rd	20
Blackbirds	21
Laundromat	23
Brief Argument for Stillness	24
Sandy	25
My Son Moves to San Antonio	26
Another Rising	27
Packing for Texas	28
Family Photo, 1981	29
Mistaken	30
Trading Rivers	31
River Notes	33
Rainwater	36
Turning in My License	37
First Texas Christmas	39
I Take Out My Slotted	41
Ode to a Singleton Sock	42
My Grandfather Leaves Bari	43
Postcard from a Past Life	44
In Central Market	46
Reveille	47
In the Mind of Water	48
Swallowed	50
Old Dog	52

Teahouse of the Texas Moon

The Jingu History	55
Teahouse of the Texas Moon	57
Mother Folds Fledglings in Wings	60
Approaching Angel Island	63
Footing	65
Tea Set Made in Occupied Japan	67
What Poetry Is	69
The Letter	71
Fuji Apples	72
The Bath	73
Gift	74
The Four Seasons	75

Speaking with Rivers

Walking the River's Edge	79
Quiddity	81
Grackles	82
Mahncke's Cypress	83
Astronomy Lesson	84
River of Dreams	85
To a Live Oak at Mission Concepción	88
Culebra de Agua	89
No Place like Home	90
Legacy of the Blue Hole	91
Hugging Skeletons	92
We Have Walked to Praise Willows	93
Speaking with Rivers	94

About the Author

Poet Is a River (excerpt)

a poet
is a river

flowing
unnoticed

caressing
stones

moving
silt from

one place
to another

From *Canto hondo / Deep Song* by Francisco X. Alarcón. © 2015 Francisco X. Alarcón. Reprinted by permission of the University of Arizona Press.

Postcard from a Past Life

The River Sings

Come.
Drop your footprints like leaves along my edge.
Let me cradle your far-flung histories
in glittering arms that sway and curve,
breathe in your blushes and shrugs,
read faces mapped by worry or wonder or joy,
fatten lungs with the hum of honeysuckle.

I sing of *abuelas* crushing saffron ears to masa,
neapolitan *papas* toiling coffee fields to earn passage,
omas building lone-star cities out of sand,
and all wanderers woven from blaring oceans
or silent island coves.
Hear my favonian song.

Sleep beside my narrow bed,
loose dreams to float with masked turtles and silken swans.
Walk beside me, all of you, into the delta of change.
Run with me. Listen, *canta!*

Inside Grand Central
one lost pigeon trapezes
in constellations

Migration

on moving from the suburbs to New York City, 2005

Overnight I go
urban from suburban,
train traveler from motorist.
Saturday we start early,
promenade for hours down Fifth, Park
to Union Square for groceries, sundries, cool Tees.
3pm, our legs rubber. In the city
that never sleeps, we do—

a silken, sink-into-our-Tempur-Pedic nap,
us two, this apartment, this dream we cram.
Awakening to dusk we behold
not finch-filled willows
but pinnacles lighted golden,
holy as church spires.

Today, on the way to Grand Central
a starling sings from his niche—
straw and trash jammed in a Starbucks sign,
resilience his tune.

Crossing 43rd

It's the man, black
watchman's cap and iPod-plugged,
who makes me feel at home.

Every day, by the Port flower stand
we pass,
oblivious, but not,
heading for work
        180°   apart.

At 7th, a zoo—
        cranes and caterpillars
construct the bones
of another skyscraper.

Beyond 6th, the man
with legs long   as linguini
bounds past
but, like Aesop's fable,
at every intersection, I catch him.

Near Madison, Fifth Church
of Christ, Scientist
gets a soul-lift.
Hardhats shoulder
steel beams like logs.

In the terminal, tangents of people
help me recall
geometry class:
how the shortest   distance between
me   and Track 23
is an impossible straight line.

Blackbirds

Stumping along blank streets,
we raise eyes to wet cement sky,
watch silhouettes of starlings pool—
black clots in leafless arteries and veins.

We drag a pale shadow, wonder:
Is it futile, this putting one foot before the other?
This battling fatigue settled marrow-deep?

Yet who can say where muddy paths
may lead? Perhaps closer
to a Nirvana not
as expected, but a new place,
a young day, some old dream.

Sidewalks like storm clouds
on wet streets, streaks of crimson
ancestors warn us

Laundromat

House rules shout from the wall:
  Be here when your laundry's done—or else!
   No pets allowed.
    Use trash cans to clean up your mess.

A Latina shows her girls the fine art of folding.
Scolding the older for sloppy creases in one breath,
she sings to piped-in soft rock in the next.
Man whose hair needs Static Guard
reads operating instructions.
People, like singleton socks, overstuff 18-pound
Wascomats to wash away life's grime.

I lug my wet load to a dryer's open mouth,
pay a quarter for each 10 minutes of hot air.
My body molds to the hard yellow seat.
Signs take no responsibility for my losses:
writing time, menses, my mother.
I glance up, scribble, glance up,
waiting for this cycle to end.

Brief Argument for Stillness

Oh, goddess Disconnect! If only I could
ignore beeps, vibrations, rings,
bow at your sandalwood altar,
create from the ethos rarified air,

venture into the cosmos to grasp
gravityless thoughts,
explore this wordless universe—
no GPS needed.

I long to pluck out rainbows, geese,
face ogres, dragons, cyber police,
heed my inner Sybil,
scrutinize orbit I travel.

No ambient noise,
just the raucous void,
the joys
of my own humming pulse.

Sandy

We wait, refrigerator packed,
water stocked,
candles and books at the ready,
phones, iPads charged.

The rain comes and we watch,
anticipate power loss
that starts four blocks south,
creeps two avenues away.
Darkness and the surge of surf
to the west, the Hudson's rage.

   How did we arrive in Oz,
   glistening technicolor in a city gone black?

On still-working TV
images of all we fear
like some prime-time horror show.
So much washed away.
In disbelief, we stab our roast beef,
helping
of guilt, jubilation, and grief
on the side.

My Son Moves to San Antonio

and it might as well be Prague.
I can't reach him by cheek,
call in a hug, or drop biscotti at his door.
Buy an iPad, he says, *then we can FaceTime.*
So I do, and he appears on screen
occasionally, but not enough.
I have to face it: time
is fleeting. So I move, too.

Another Rising

Sky dark as coffee.
You dress by TV's blue glow,
listen to news drone on. Time to go,
grab your bag, head for the bus stop
one block away.
Still sleepy, you wait as sky grows pink and gold.
Perfectly clear:
there's only this morning
breaking   wide open
and full of promise.

Packing for Texas

What we don't pack:
set of dishes missing one,
sturdy plastic measuring cups,
T-shirts mapping where we've been,
our lumpy brown couch,
lopsided torchière,
bed we bought when we moved to the city.
Boxes of sentiment stored for a decade,
Central Park—
all gone to reduce movers' fees.

What we take: my desert-island book stash,
your desk,
drafts of my half-cooked poems,
memories of trips to Friedman for art supplies
and your Faicco market runs.

There's just so much a person can take!
Have to make
room for the new,
our life to move in
whichever direction we choose.

Family Photo, 1981

My mother's dress is patterned like a blizzard.
Her smile spreads like good news. She holds
my son in his Crayola colors. Grandfather
clock is stopped at 3:13.

And she who snaps the shot resembles both—
grandmother and grandson linked
that cold March afternoon—in flash
reflecting on her glasses, his drooled chin.

Outside the photo's frame,
her kisses on pink cheek, how he tugs her
auburn hair. And when she goes, his chubby hand,
nose pressed to frigid pane. My hand

wipes wetness he imprints on glass,
scours dishes piled in sink,
clicks TV black.
Near midnight, the jarring ring.

My husband grabs the phone.
A thrust of words and light.
Camera squinting
from my dresser top.

The clock chimes slow and long.
I stumble out of bed, bare feet
pounding down the hall
hungry for the breathing of my son.

Mistaken

Only in the dead of night my mother,
lost to the seismic quake in her chest,
returns to my unbridled delight.

Not gone at all.
She wastes no time in preparing
chicken pot pie,
lasagna,
a big, thick steak.
From head of the table she pours wine.
In our gold-washed room, I crouch at her side,
press my face against her flushed cheek,
inhale honeysuckle,
feel in her kiss the soft landing of a Monarch.

And my family, we—
all laughing and talking—reach
for seconds, for one more hunk
of honeyed bread from her hands.
Greedy, we demand more
and she hurries to the kitchen,

doesn't return. A cloud blinds us.
In the darkness, we keen like wolves.

And then I awake,
the aftershock
more shattering than the dream.

Trading Rivers

I forfeit the Hudson,
wild child I discovered like
the Dutchman seeking
      somewhere else.

      Hiking beside her
ice floes, ideas freeze.
I shelter under snow-enameled pines
      until crocus's violet thaw.

      Mi nuevo río me habla en español,
wears ripples like ruffles on a fiesta dress
swallows red-eared turtles beneath sun-baked skin.
      Cypress and palm guard her.

      I move like a river,
roving, blank-eyed
ear attuned to currents.
      I translate.

Iridescent sky
cabbing a Texas highway
I snare shooting star

River Notes

1.
Moonlight shines like schools
of neons
except on moonless nights.

2.
Homely, the color of mud.
You call this a river?

3.
Torrential rains bloat
sidewalks, fill roads with debris.
Stay home.

4.
Even your river teems
with deluge of stories, legends, sprites,
enough to make Noah quake.

5.
Water snakes, rattlers, diamondbacks.
Mallards, Muscovies, pom-poms.
Cormorants, egrets, white-billed coots.
Lizards, red-eared turtles, frogs.
Fiesta!

6.
The page a spillway,
what rushes into my head caught
then disappears.

7.
Rocking the cradle of civilization.
Deltas. Sources of irrigation, power,

transportation, shipping, protection.
Grande wailing wall.

8.
Down under:
   Murray-Darling, Murrumbidgee, Lachlan.
Underworld:
   Styx, hatred. Acheron, woe. Lethe, amnesia.
   Phlegethon, fire. Cocytus, wailing.
   Pay the coin or remain unburied.

9.
Movement mysterious as breath calms me.

Shock of bluebonnets
a Ladybird's legacy—
periwinkle lakes

Rainwater

*Golden Shovel poem mining William Carlos
Williams's "The Red Wheelbarrow"*

I love you so-
-and-so, and so much
that my breath depends
on if you choose to rise upon
the break of day or stay a
secret buried in red
clay. I will collect your bones and wheel
them in a narrow barrow
until by mist they're glazed.
But who to talk with?
One stranger overcome by rain?
Meet me down by the water-
wheel beside
river, below moon so bright, it's the
North Star that glows white
and in the shadows, ghostly chickens.

Turning in My License

My permit from New York
to motor its highways and byways,
quaff a Guinness stout,
board domestic flights westward.

Today, without question, I tender it,
squirrelly photo, seal of the Empire State.
Laminated card that pulls,
I admit, on heartstrings

as the Public Safety rep
requests it, along with passport,
proof of insurance, utility bill,
and faded Social Security card.

The only doc not returned.
Give it back, I want to shout.
It's where I'm from, who I am!
Instead I accept

temporary Texas license—
flimsy photocopy, new snapshot
of an older me,
shell-shocked.

Texas December
icy blade of butcher's steel
sharp to the bone—why?

First Texas Christmas

December 2017

Feelings jambalaya-mixed
I unwrap balls treasured for decades

popsicle-stick sled
glittering pine cones

stardusted
by our son's small hands

my mother's (last unbroken)
ornament of glass

beaded bell your father made
after he took ill.

Years, bubble-wrapped and boxed
from New York

brighter than the tree's LED lights.
I miss East Coast cold

perennial wish for Christmas white
the family savoring seven fishes

for 65 years.
I check recipes, ancient and coffee-stained

bake the cream cheese cookies of my childhood.
Each tradition's core, a seed

we wait
to flower like prickly pear.

Gifts nestled beneath the tree,
like all of us, dressed

and ready
to rip.

I Take Out My Slotted

aluminum spoon,
sift out stones and twigs from soil,
try to re-pot the spider
plant you gave me five years ago.

It is suffocating:
too big for the too-small pot,
roots compacted like recycled tin cans,
leaf tips edged in brown,
sparse minerals,
not enough water,
too little dirt.

Wouldn't it be easier to let it go?
Return the remaining soil to the yard
and start over with a new leafy fern?

I push my spoon deep into the ground,
loosen a small pile of earth,
shake it like the powdered sugar
you loved on pancakes,
toss pebbles back.

With my hands
I sift soil
enough to fill an empty pot half-way,
position the old plant
in its new home,
patting, adding,
watering,
waiting on blooms.

Ode to a Singleton Sock

with apologies to Pablo Neruda

I loathe the bite of cold linoleum on feet.
The chill numbs toes and even shins.
Rummaging drawer
I look for crackling heat,
find cherished maroon and purple sock
festooned in polka dots—
but where is mate?
Did it walk away, angry at something I said?

I could choose grey wool
or the blue argyles, but no. Colors too cool.
I need a warm cave for soles to spelunk.
Spotted sock I hold in hand would do,
but on which foot?
If I sit on the left, as if hatching an egg,
I could pull soft cap over my right—
then switch.

Will the uncovered tootsie fall asleep?
Will I even be able to unbend my knee?
And as evening gets late, I wonder,
where would I be
without my mate?

My Grandfather Leaves Bari

Italy to Argentine plantation.
He measures days in coffee beans,
earns passage to Ellis,
two *bambinos*, an olive-skinned wife.
Small New Rochelle grocery store,
later, room
in his oldest child's home.

In no time flat, white haired,
cardiganed, round as a pumpkin.
Inside one pocket, his silver fob
in the other, crumbs for the birds.

Fractured English
embarrasses. But I could watch
him tend tomatoes and mint,
his shadow lengthening, for hours.

He plants a peach pit
to show me how patience pays off—
though never sees it sprout.

Comfort comes in vinyl arias
like spun sugar, sung
in the heartland language he never leaves behind.

Postcard from a Past Life

Long
past lavender waters
some faraway place—Belarus?
Seoul-baring in Korea?
As if God doesn't exist, only the river
reflecting
sugar-coated stones.

Ambiguity everywhere:
twins unalike
as popcorn and lead,
ebony and white.
All is not darkness.
Even at midnight roses
glow ROYGBIV rainbows in the shadows.
The magic in the mystery casts
incomparable light.

Naples rain spills
cold on American skin
wine and crusty bread

In Central Market

Papples, lematoes, pluots,
tangelos, blood limes.
I think I hear whispers—
Who am I?

Me? I'm a jumble, too:
graying crone
eyes nested in crow's feet,
plucky inner child
calendar can't explain, yet
triumphant lipstick glaze.

Mutt of blood lines—
part Neapolitan, part Barese,
a schmal bit of Schnitzel—
just as that cronut
lures me

to bakery case,
donut kin—
crossbreed,
and like me,
perfectly iced.

Reveille

Our bodies have more
issues
but in our head we're stuck
at 23.
By the sink
the dishes, warm and soapy
in my hands.
You
sneak up,
breath hot,
body pressed,
hands still hungry—
this evening's reveille:
      wake up
              go now to bed.

In the Mind of Water

after a performance by Béla Fleck and Abigail Washburn

Run.
Change paths
overflow banks
rush river rocks
trickle through cypress roots.

Intricate banjo currents
shivery and warm
twisted tributaries
two tunes skipping like stones.

River breeze rises falls.
Your call: wild thumb-thump-thump
against lacquered head.
We respond:
stomp
clap
jump into the music's stream
reborn.

Peonies ripen
at first light petals gather
my table covered

Swallowed

Pink July morning, heat dense
as unleavened dough.
From balcony, shifting Texas sky, slip
of lemon-twist moon,
distant piccolo of birds.
Reverie

interruptus:
four gaping dumpsters
like soldiers at rest
in the lot below.
I nudge my gaze
away, but you know
how it is—can't keep your tongue
from tooth that aches.

Startled:
camouflage of swallows—
landing, calling cadence,
marching about the offending bins—
steal

scraps, disband thoughts
to fly in resplendent air
the bad with the good,
stand watch on a day
I refuse to trash.

Burnished camellia
ribbons offered to the sun
unaware I watch

Old Dog

I circle in familiar dance,
greet at the door,
spring at every chance to please
with how much I know.
Expect pat on the head,
wag tail at their *good girl!*

I'm unaware how blindly I pad about:
furniture is moved,
shape in the mirror strange.

Words not in my routine
confuse. I search the eyes I trust.
Is this what you want me to do?

Old or not, it's time
to heed what's said,
learn the new trick,
catch the scent of change.
Roll over.

Teahouse of the Texas Moon

The Jingu History

Japanese immigrants Kimi and Miyoshi Jingu left California for San Antonio in the early 1900s. The city invited Kimi, a tea purveyor and artist, to reside in and host the city's lush new Japanese Tea Garden. Under his management, the Tea Garden became a popular attraction where Miyoshi and her daughters performed tea ceremony and Ikebana demonstrations in traditional Japanese dress. In the public school system, the family's eight children excelled in sports, arts, and academics. The Jingus were, as the local newspaper proclaimed, "one of San Antonio's unique assets."

When Pearl Harbor happened in 1942, the high esteem changed overnight. The Jingus were classified as "enemy aliens" despite Kimi's record as a U.S. Army veteran, his long-time friendship with the mayor, a son's enlistment in the Army, and daughters who volunteered for Civil Defense. They were ousted from their home, which the city quickly renamed the Chinese Tea Garden.

Somehow they survived and triumphed. The poems in this section are dedicated to their granddaughter, Nancy, and to everyone in the Jingu family.

Teahouse of the Texas Moon

There is nothing you can think that is not the moon.
       —Matsuo Basho

Your silvered glow, San Antonio moon,
spills like a billion stars.

Under your cool fire,
I count hours, if lucky, days.
Where will we go?
That faraway city,
named for crystal
but adorned with barbed wire?

My eight young
who yesterday splashed among lily pads
long for their artist father
as if five years passed in five nights.
Beneath your piercing eye, I lie:
  We will be all right.

What to take? My mother's kimono of red silk?
To warm us, some earthy matcha tea?
This small painting by Kimi, snow
white peony luminous through cobalt glaze?
Or from our pond, lotus
like a sleeping angel?

Gratitude of guests now gone?
  This tea is refreshing, Miyoshi.
    Your children, so sweet—especially Mabel.

In December's damp chill,
I pray to you, gibbous god,
my hope thin as rice paper.
Let me be quicksilver,

shift, change,
move as fluidly as indigo watercolor.

Under your lunar light,
Pearl Harbor.
Will mercy rise
for those who shout at us
    Leave now—and don't look back?

Wandering Sister, who never failed
my sky-bent prayers,
will you return to fullness?
Seed the river's face with iridescent pearls?

Matcha leaves float
caterpillars sprout wings
we drink western breeze

Mother Folds Fledglings in Wings

Origami takes patience, time.
Let me show you how
to make *tsuru*.
First, clear your mind.
Be quiet, calm.

This is the *kami*, thin
and easy to crease.
Solid or striped—
which pleases?
Be sure the side that shines
like bright sun faces you.

Turn down the top edge
to meet the bottom
in *mountain fold*.
See how the paper stands
like a San Gabriel peak?
Now crease with your nail.
Very good.

Here's how to make a *valley fold*:
right to left, vertically, like this,
then crease.
No, it doesn't look like a crane yet.
Just stay with me.

Diagonal fold next.
Crease again.
Now the other side.
Watch me and follow—
from sharp angles we shape
head, body, tail, wings.
Soon our cranes will be done.

It's said if you form one
thousand *tsuru,*
make a wish after each,
your heart's desire will come true.

[Fragile crane,
carry us from Los Angeles
to Texas-wide plains.
Let us reach up, shape a new moon.]

There! Isn't it sweet?
Pull. Its wings, fluttering fans.
Listen! Like a heart you can hear them beat.

Seventeen heartbeats
willows weep deep into pond
koi move on, feed

Approaching Angel Island

Will I see castles rising from clouds?
Sweep of wings through diffused light shafts?

Feel invisible heft
of guardian to guide me?

Tendon-tired and thirsty for air
sibilance of sequoia

embrace of yellow-
haloed (not red) sun

azure ocean's cleansing waves.
I dream of palms, divine smiles

coalescence of miso and burgers
sticky rice and fries

matcha and milkshakes
soon to be mine.

Seed-head mother moon
spilling a million white spores
across midnight sky

Footing

So many rocks.
So much sepia-hued hope
in the photo.

Proud papa, clad in shirt and tie,
arms drape across slight
shoulders of two young sons.

Even the dog
stands erect
below tea garden sign

telling us
in two languages
where they are.

Limestone idyll
Kimi helped build,
cocoon for growing family.

Early stop
on shifting timeline
he can't keep pace.

Beneath his right heel
you see the foundation
crack.

Stealth moon tiptoes in
beams like blue dandelion fluff
we watch where we step

Tea Set Made in Occupied Japan

In my mother's breakfront,
plates and porcelain cups
royal gold-etched bamboo,
celadon leaves, eggshell glaze.
On bottoms and backs, insignia elephant head.
Made in Occupied Japan.

Cool ridges sensual
painted by unknown hands
under suffering we can not conceive.
Dishes that held sweetmeats,
cups filled with oolong.
Whose scent do they carry?
Whose touch?

Despite her own occupation—
enduring untrue spouse, aging parents,
three taxing children—
she practiced art her way,
sweeping brush strokes on rock-garden canvas,
scarlet roses, white candy tuft,
offering tea her comfort.

Artisan with sauces, healing
as religion
until her heart burst.
This set now occupies the hutch
of a daughter who pines
to share one final cup.

From unknown river
Sirens croon long keening songs
should we turn and run?

What Poetry Is

Usual garden walk. Unusual day.
Cobalt, celadon, rose. Wind blows,
pond ripples, koi swirl.
Trees sing—
sibilant, uplifting.

Transported,
gaze at leaves like gliders and sole
egret a-wing on breeze guiding its flight
like poetry—letting the draft write itself.

Sun lavas asphalt
heat rises, herons retreat
steam fogs my glasses

The Letter

after dry point/aquatint by Mary Cassat, 1890-91

Early-century woman, home
her domain. Coal
hair knotted loose,
wisps like writing
on her forehead's scroll,
porcelain geisha-like skin.
        Dress printed ochre
        on peacock blue silk.
        At her neck, cravat a blooming rose.
Fluid strokes cover walls,
bamboo leaves scattered like footprints of herons.
At flattened desk, her page is full:
        pining for aged parents?
        painting for them her western life?
How hard to belong where you aren't from.

Tongue to glue, she accepts
that families stick together. That blood
is forever
        thick and red as setting sun.

Fuji Apples

He walks away
from the basket,
snaps plastic bags like towels
just pulled from the line.

He palms apples, speckled,
red-freckled from the sun.
One by one he gathers them
for her.

Somehow it's the same
as taking home
Mount Fuji—
just because she wants it.

The Bath

after dry point/aquatint by Mary Cassat, 1890-91

She embraces chubby child
like a rescued wren.
Evening ritual:
warm bath drawn
recalling oceans, rivers crossed.
Water tested
on her own flesh.
Soap caresses skin tender as a kiss.
Thick towel blots dry.

The two, jewel-like,
the moment
so dazzling it blinds.

Gift

on receiving a cherished scarf from her husband

Liquid silk
illumined by
waterlilies, reeds.
Vintage kimonos
navy, gold-
patched stories
once worn
by women.
This woman
drapes it
like arms
shielding cold
holding dreams.

The Four Seasons

*for Nancy Enkoji, after the name of watercolor mural
by her grandfather Kimi*

In maze of garden paths
ours have crossed.
I hear your grandmother calling—
James, Kimi, Rae,
Lillian, Mary, Helen,
Ruth, Mabel your mother.
Laughter like moss in spring trees.

Here I see paradise in her eyes,
waves of summer blooms thick
with her honeyed poems.
Rows of stones like ivory
surround lily pond,
crown the high walls
by waterfall's autumn rush.
In winter, I sit where guests took
matcha from her hands.

Inside
on Bamboo Room ceiling,
your grandfather's mural,
heavenly pastiche in four panels,
displaced by season of ill will.
Above me now
its soul restored,
its beauty, by your hand,
revived.

Speaking with Rivers

Walking the River's Edge

Mighty agaves rise from dry clay
their splayed hands skimming the sky.
Lily-white air and coral sun fire.
Beside the river's riffles, runs, and pools
cacti with coxcomb blooms festoon my walk.
Despite scarce water, spiny xerophytes
from another place thrive.
I, a transplant too,
like the prickly pear,
shallow-rooted, thick-skinned,
inspired.

Tai chi veterans
arms like mighty oak branches
I rest in their shade

Quiddity

I want the unadulterated you
the you the sun rises on
you cast in cool moon blue
you steady as the Hudson.

I need the veil dislodged
revealing the bubbling
quiddity of you.

I reach to finger fabric
texture, weave
the selvage, seam
thread that binds
the give and take
the give.

Grackles

In Mexican legend, you are *zanates*.
No voice of your own, you steal
the sea turtle's songs
of seven passions: love,
hate, courage, fear,
sadness, anger, joy.

Here in San Antonio
your racket frazzles nerves.
A street gang
keeled tails like scroungy rakes
violet shadows clouding phone wires.

Beneath your yellow eye
I trek *Paseo del Río,*
spy single viridian
hummingbird
hovering like a Giotto cherub
wingbeats fanning the air
shimmering on nectar.

Still your rusty-gate song, black nacre coat,
call me.
Unlikely winged thief
come to fly me home.

Mahncke's Cypress

or how a City Parks Commissioner responds to the 1819
San Antonio River flood

Fearing another uprising
  of murderous floodwaters
    of citizens' ire at lost children, at the downing
    of two sacred willows weeping on the banks,
Ludwig Mahncke paid

for 300 saplings
(from his own purse)
dislodged from Guadalupe and Cypress Creeks
    cradled in wet hay
      planted by Navarro and Mill Bridge
      where the river bends.

Mahncke's cypress
promising as his own children.
Roots to anchor soil.
Branches
to reach for stars.

Astronomy Lesson

Galaxies circle me
   a point in time

compilation of granite, moonbeams, sunstorms
   small pebble tossed into black river

of the universe.
   What hides in these concentric springs?

What silence shatters my ear?
   What debris careens and tatters?

And what of me is left to return—
   lone shining gift

I throw back in gratitude
   to midnight sky—

my platinum earthly star
    longing for crystalline constellations?

River of Dreams

–Los padres
Like a prayer in darkness, we steal across narrow pass
family in hand, impassable as linked fence
eyes like owls, legs moving wide and quiet like a heron
toward the unknown shore, worrying what's next.

We leave behind: certainty of hardship, poverty, despair,
las abuelas y los tíos.
On the other side: hope, hard work, uncertainty,
    muchos sueños para nuestros hijos
poised to fan out like morning
glories in warmth of a new sun.

We take our chances.

—*Los políticos*
We hold 800,000 fates in our soiled hands.
Some of us want our nation to thrive
to keep dreams alive.
Some want to wall them all out.
Divided as partisan river

we must build a bridge.

—*Los soñadores*
America, only country we recall.
We learn English, translate for our parents
the language, the ways.

A dark threat
circles like a vulture just above,
of deportation across the long river
where we would be strangers.
Miracle: we are called legal—for a time,

earn degrees, sit at desks, breathe.

This life, chosen by our parents,
we have made our own.
Citizens in every sense but one.
If we keep dreaming, hope will rise like mist.

We work, watch, persist.

El río de invierno
la misma cara de julio, huesos helados

vivir o morir?

The winter river
same July face, icy
  bones
live or die?

To a Live Oak at Mission Concepción

October. Your leafed cathedral dome
dapples my bare arms gold,
filters shimmering threads of light.

Like my ancient grandfather's knuckles
arthritic roots rise sapless from soil
knobby and arched in prayer.

Leaning against your umber trunk
your husk fatted by rings, concentric
around a common soul. I breathe in.

Two campanile bells call me to matins
and the ghosts, sowing, painting, working, crushing
in the hushed air.

Here I stand, a single acorn
humbled, beholden, open
and rooted in awe.

Culebra de Agua

*for the children who died in the San Antonio River flood
of July 5, 1819*

Another day near Yanaguana.
We splash and play on floating footbridge
even in dashing rain.
Then San Pedro overflows,
streams flash.
Surge of Olmos Creek

like burning lava—
culebra de agua sweeps
our small brown bodies,
indistinct from drowned dogs,
grieving wagons,
downed oaks.

We long
sleep beside mastodon bones
until another July's currents
snake,
undulate, kiss stones and once
again
with the river, our spirits rise.

No Place like Home

Fabled ache that claws at thumping heart till all four quadrants bleed, or eludes, persistent as motile midway ducks. Where you sprout leaves or lean as if your green life depended on beating *sol* —emotional bicoastal. Ellis. Angel. Island hug or choke hold? Like homing pigeon, do you fly back? East? West? Edge closer to roots? Hiroshima after 75 years? Naples…a little village near? Damascus, what's left of it? Sanctuaried in cactus-scorched, lone-star middle earth. Your own diaspora. Where does it end? Can you find that place, once and for all, domiciled deep within bristling hollow bones?

Legacy of the Blue Hole

*a 1970s Olmos Dam excavation uncovers ancient
Payayan burial site*

Good spot to stop, camp, barter, hunt,
for purification, trek
the Sacred Circle,
16 springs that defy
cactus-choked heat.

By sky-painted waters
we bury our dead
with shards
of shell and bone,
antlers of the white-tail deer.

The Blue Panther thrived here.
Chased Water Bird who released
from widespread wings
aqua crystals
to quench the jagged land—

and the river rose.
We beat the drum for our beloveds
shimmering in rain
flying to azure light.

Hugging Skeletons

an anniversary poem

> *There has not been a double burial found in the Neolithic period, much less two people hugging.*
> —Elena Menotti, Italian archeologist

They remind me of us
these two from Mantova,
only thinner,
arms linked like a fence,
legs intertwined like ivy.
Fetally curled and facing each other
two bodies, one bony heart.

I can't help but wonder
if they were positioned for pillow talk,
if his fingers brushed her cheek,
if like me, she
had cold feet.

Their teeth mostly intact…not worn down.
Well, that lets us out—you
with your TMJ
me with more silver than Mexico.

Intruders of the 5,000-year-old bed gasp.
  I've never been so moved, said the one who led the dig.
  This is the discovery of something special.

But the more I study their photo
the more they look ordinary.
Tonight I admire your angular jaw,
fine span of your hands
as we warm to blankets and body heat.

Tonight I grasp
archeology like never before.

We Have Walked to Praise Willows

Like we do,
    these trees circle Harlem Meer
        wild-haired girls leaning into lake
            to admire their own reflections.

He watches their lanky arms sway in lazy breeze,
    verdant bowers startling against cobalt.
        Stepping from the path, he frees
            stagnant October leaves into piles of sunbeams.

Against the moon he throws handfuls
    trying to catch a few
        that weave and fall back
            like drunken fireflies.

Still as midnight,
    I'm stuck to the path.
        He tosses
            a handful my way.

Breaking one hosanna-thin branch—
    two leaves caught like minnows
        on a single hook—
            he presses it into my wild, hungry hand.

Speaking with Rivers

with gratitude to Langston Hughes

Rivers have known me.
  Rivers ages and ages old.
    Rivers venerable as earth's crust.

    I've tread narrow wanderings of the Bronx River.
     I've watched dawn make the Hudson blush.
      Near Tom's River under the brightest star
    succumbed to sleep.
    I've caught the San Antonio singing to me
  in Spanish
near sites where Payayans shared sacred myths like masa.
Unworthy of rivers, I gaze at their forgiving liquid-
  constellation faces.

  Many rivers I've called my own
    others have murmured my name.
     I've grown ragged like rivers
    welcome their wisdom in my blood.
   They seek answers
  and there is no question
the river will save us.

Acknowledgments

With grateful acknowledgment to the following publications in which these poems (some in earlier versions) first appeared:

Adanna: "Quiddity"
Indiana Voice Journal: "Burnished camellia," "Peonies ripen" and "Tai chi veterans"
Poeming Pigeon: "Ode to a Singleton Sock"

Bearing the Mask: Southwestern Persona Poems (Dos Gatos Press, 2016): "Teahouse of the Texas Moon"
Cow Tippers, Linda Simone (Shadows Ink Publications, 2006): "Blackbirds" and "Laundromat"
Exposure XV: "Family Photo, 1981"
Let the Poets Speak (Greenburgh Arts and Culture, 2007): "Hugging Skeletons"
The Crafty Poet: A Portable Poetry Workshop, Ed. Diane Lockward (Wind Publications, 2013): "Mistaken"
The Crafty Poet II: A Portable Poetry Workshop, Ed. Diane Lockward (Terrapin Press, 2016): "We Have Walked to Praise Willows"
The Texas Poetry Calendar 2017 (Dos Gatos Press): "Grackles"

Love Poems to San Antonio (signature initiative of San Antonio Poet Laureate Laurie Ann Guerrero): "The River Sings" and "To a Live Oak at Mission Concepción"
Norwalk, CT Bus Project: "Another Rising"
San Antonio Express-News: "In Central Market" and "Walking the River's Edge"
Thirty Poems for the Tricentennial: A Poetic Legacy: "Legacy of the Blue Hole"

VIA Poetry on the Move: "My Son Moves to San Antonio"

"Mistaken" and "Hugging Skeletons" also appeared in *Archeology,* Linda Simone (Flutter Press, 2014)

With gratitude…

To my family and friends for their love and support during the writing of this book, particularly Joe, always my first listener, and my Sapphires, Sarah Bracey White, Terry Dugan, and especially Ann Cefola, without whom this manuscript would not have been birthed.

To Karen Kelsay for her patience during the editing and publication process. And finally, to the late Thomas Lux for teaching me that the rigorous process of revision is what makes a poem come to life.

About the Author

Linda Simone is the author of *Archeology* (Flutter Press), *Cow Tippers* (Shadow Ink Publications), and a children's book, *Moon: A Poem* (Richard C. Owen Publishers). Her poems have been widely published in journals and anthologies, most recently in the anthologies, *Carnival* and *Bearing the Mask: Southwestern Persona Poems.* "The Stubborn Poem: Tackle or Trash?" is forthcoming in the anthology *Far Villages: Welcome Essays for New and Beginner Poets* (Black Lawrence Press). Her work was selected for inclusion in San Antonio's *Thirty Poems for the Tricentennial: A Poetic Legacy,* as well as in San Antonio Poet Laureate Laurie Ann Guerrero's signature poetry project, and on public buses in San Antonio and Norwalk, CT. A native New Yorker, Simone now lives in San Antonio.

www.lindasimone.com.

www.ingramcontent.com/pod-product-compliance
Lightning Source LLC
Chambersburg PA
CBHW031000090426
42737CB00007B/613